LIVEWIRE PLAYS

The Trip

Peter Leigh

Acknowledgements
Illustrations: Jim Eldridge.
Cover: Dave Smith / Organisation.

Orders: please contact Bookpoint Ltd, 39 Milton Park, Abingdon, Oxon OX14
4TD. Telephone: (44) 01235 400414, Fax: (44) 01235 400454. Lines are open
from 9.00–6.00, Monday to Saturday, with a 24 hour message answering
service. Email address: orders@bookpoint.co.uk

British Library Cataloguing in Publication Data
A catalogue record for this title is available from The British Library

ISBN 0 340 72102 2

First published 1998
Impression number   10 9 8 7 6 5 4 3 2 1
Year   2003 2002 2001 2000 1999 1998

Typeset by Fakenham Photosetting Ltd, Fakenham, Norfolk.
Printed in Great Britain for Hodder & Stoughton Educational, a division of
Hodder Headline Plc, 338 Euston Road, London NW1 3BH by Athenaeum
Press Ltd, Gateshead, Tyne & Wear.

About the play

The People

Mr Jones, a young teacher

Amy

Debbie

Adam

Kevin

Emma

other members of the class

a Policeman

What's Happening

A Year 9 class are waiting by the school minibus.
They are going on a trip to Denton Park,
a large amusement park.
***Mr Jones**, the teacher in charge,*
is walking towards them.

Act 1

Kevin	Hurry up, sir! We'll be late.
Amy	Come on, sir.
Mr Jones	What's all the panic?
	There's no rush.
Debbie	If you don't get there early
	you have to queue for hours.
Mr Jones	Oh, there's plenty of time.
	You're never as keen as this
	to get to my lesson.

He reaches the minibus,
and opens the doors.

Now just stand back,
and don't all rush at once.

The kids charge for the doors,
pushing and shoving.

Mr Jones   I said don't all rush at once.

Adam   I want the back …

Kevin   The back seat's mine …

Adam   No it isn't …

Debbie   Me and Amy always
                       sit next to each other.

Amy   We were here first …

Adam   Too bad! Kevin was saving it
                       for me. Weren't you Kev?

Kevin   No!

Adam   See! There we are!

Amy   No, you're not. You're sitting next
                       to sir.

Kevin   No, I'm not. I'm …

Mr Jones   (*Sticking his head through the*
                       back door)
                       Right!

Out!

All of you!

Now!

Everyone   Oh sir, I've just sat down ...

It's not my fault, sir ...

Sir, we'll be late ...

Mr Jones   Out!

(*They come out grumbling*)

Right!

Is that how you should behave on a bus?

Silence

Is it?

Everyone   No sir!

| **Mr Jones** | Good!
| | Because if it is,
| | we shall not be going to
| | Denton Park today!
| | We shall be sitting in class
| | all day doing Maths!
| | Do you want that?
| | Do you?
| **Everyone** | No sir!

Mr Jones	Good. Let's try again then,
	shall we?
	We'll get on the minibus
	like sensible people –
	we'll find a seat –
	we'll sit down quietly –
	and we'll put our seat belts on,
	because this minibus
	doesn't go anywhere
	unless everyone is belted up.
	OK?
Everyone	Yes sir.
Mr Jones	Right then.
	Get in.

They get in quietly.
Mr Jones *closes the door*
behind them,
and gets into the driver's seat.

Mr Jones	Now keep still while I count you.
	One, two, three, four ...
Adam	Sir, someone's stolen my bag!
Mr Jones	Sit down, Adam!
Adam	Who's got my bag?
Kevin	I haven't got your bag.
Adam	It's got my sandwiches in it.
Kevin	I don't want your smelly
	sandwiches.
Mr Jones	Adam! Will you sit down!
	I've lost count now.
Adam	Well, someone's got my bag.
	(*To* **Amy**)
	Have you got my bag?
Amy	I wouldn't touch your bag.
	I might catch something.
Mr Jones	(*In a resigned voice*)
	All right then, Adam.
	Who's got Adam's bag?

(Silence)

Mr Jones   You see, Adam.

No-one's got your bag.

You must have forgotten it.

Adam   But it was here a minute ago.

Mr Jones   Well, too bad.

No-one has got it, and ...

(Pause)

Adam?

Adam   Yes, sir?

Mr Jones   Is your bag blue with red pockets?

Adam   Yes, sir. Have you got it?

Mr Jones   What is that under your seat?

Adam   Oh yes ...

Mr Jones   Oh yes indeed!

Adam, you know those two things

called eyes?

Adam	Yes sir.
Mr Jones	They're not just to hold your eyebrows up, they have a use.
Adam	Yes sir.
Mr Jones	So USE them! Right. Where were we? One, two, three ...
Amy	Sir! Sir!
Mr Jones	What is it now, Amy?
Amy	Sir, where's Emma? Emma's supposed to be coming.
Mr Jones	No Amy. Emma is not coming.
Amy	Yes she is, sir. She told me she was.

Mr Jones	No she isn't, Amy.
	Not after last time!
Amy	But sir, that's not fair.
	That wasn't Emma's fault.
Mr Jones	That's not what I thought.
Amy	It was that boy from
	the other school.
	It was him that did it.
Mr Jones	Too bad.
Amy	She didn't know
	what he was going to do
	once they got into the tunnel.
Mr Jones	Look, I'm sorry, but get this clear!
	Emma is not going on this trip,
	or any other for that matter.
	Now, let's get on.
	One, two, three ...

Everyone (*Getting out of their seats and crowding round Amy*) What happened Amy? … What did she do? … Tell us …

Amy Well, Emma met this boy on the Ghost Train, and when they went into the tunnel … (*She starts to giggle*)

Everyone	(*Eagerly*)
	Yes?
Mr Jones	Back to your seats all of you.
	Amy, be quiet.
	We don't want to hear
	any more about it.
Kevin	Oh sir ...
Mr Jones	If you don't sit down now,
	and stay sat down,
	and stay belted up,
	that is it!
	End of trip – Understand?

(*Silence*)

Right!
One, two, three ... eleven, twelve!
That's it! Let's go!

Act 2

On the minibus half an hour later.

Mr Jones *is driving.*

Everyone is quiet.

Some are nearly asleep.

Amy *and* **Debbie** *are*

on the seat behind **Mr Jones**.

Amy	You know Mr Jones?
Debbie	What about him?
Amy	He likes Miss Smith.
Debbie	So?
Amy	You know, he *likes* her.
Debbie	How do you know that?
Amy	My sister saw them together in town.

Debbie	That doesn't mean anything.
	I saw you and Kevin together
	in town.
	That doesn't mean you were
	together.
Amy	I'm going to ask him.
Debbie	Amy, that's rude!
Amy	No, it's not! I'm only asking.

She kneels up on the seat behind
Mr Jones

	Sir?
Mr Jones	Yes, Amy?
Amy	You like Miss Smith, don't you sir?
Mr Jones	(*Taken aback*)
	What?
Amy	Miss Smith. You like her?
Mr Jones	Well ... er ...
	Of course I like Miss Smith.
	She's a very good teacher.

Amy	No, not like that.
	I mean you *like* her.
Mr Jones	Amy! What do you mean by that?
Amy	You know sir.
	I'm only asking.
Mr Jones	What business is it of yours?
	It has nothing to do with you
	whether I *like* Miss Smith or not.
	Is that clear?
Amy	Yes sir.
Mr Jones	If two teachers *like* each other,
	then it's their business,
	and it's very rude of you
	to poke your nose into it.
Amy	Yes sir.
Mr Jones	And in any case,
	what are you doing out of
	your seat?
	Sit down, Amy.

Amy	Yes sir.
Mr Jones	Put your seat belt back on,
	and don't disturb me again.
Amy	Yes sir.

She slides back down the seat,
*and turns to **Debbie**.*

	I told you he liked her!
Adam	Sir, sir!
Mr Jones	What is it, Adam?
Adam	It's Kevin, sir.
	He's feeling sick.
Mr Jones	Too bad! Tell him to hold it in.
Adam	But he is, sir.
	He's gone all green.
	You'd better stop sir.
Mr Jones	I can't stop now,
	I'm on the motorway.

Adam	He's going to be sick sir, over everybody!
Mr Jones	Well, open the window!

Adam opens the window.

| **Kevin** | That's better. |

A wasp flies in!

| **Adam** | WASP! WASP!
Danger! |

Everyone squeals, and dives for cover.
The bus lurches from side to side.

Mr Jones	Sit down, everyone! Stay still!
Debbie	But sir, it's a wasp!

Mr Jones	Just ignore it.
	It won't hurt you,
	if you don't hurt it.
Debbie	That's what my mum said,
	and she got stung three times!
Mr Jones	It's only a wasp.
	Just forget about it.
Debbie	But sir, it's gone in your hair.
Mr Jones	WHAT!!!
	Get it out! Get it out!
	Mr Jones shakes his head,
	and tries to brush the wasp off.
	The bus swerves even more.
Adam	It's gone on the window.
	I'll get it!
	He takes off one of his boots.

Mr Jones   No Adam, not with that!

Too late!
Adam *smacks the wasp with his boot.*
There is a great crack,
and the glass shatters.

Adam   Oops! Sorry!

Mr Jones	Oh great! Just great!
	Well done, Adam!
	Very well done!
Adam	Well I couldn't help it ...

*Mr Jones pulls the minibus
onto the hard shoulder.
He gets out, and opens the doors.*

All right, everybody out!
Let's see the damage.

*Everyone comes out grumbling.
'Adam you idiot!'
'You prat!' etc, etc.*

Adam   It wasn't my fault ...

Mr Jones   All right, Adam! Never mind now.
Let's just have a look.

When everyone is out,
Mr Jones *climbs in to have a look.*
He doesn't notice that
they start to wander off.
He speaks to himself.

What do we do now?
It's only ten minutes to
Denton Park.
If we sweep up the worst,
then we can get it mended
while we're there.
Yes, that's best . . .
Oh no! What now?

A police car pulls in
behind the minibus.
It has all its lights flashing.
*A **Policeman** gets out.*
He comes up to the minibus,
*just as **Mr Jones** is getting out.*

Policeman Is this your minibus, sir?

Mr Jones Yes, officer! Er ... that is ... no!
It belongs to the school.
But I'm in charge of it.

Policeman I see, sir.
And are you also in charge of
these kids?

Mr Jones Yes, we're on a trip.
We're going to Denton Park.

Policeman Well, don't you think you better
get them under control?

Mr Jones   What? What do you mean?
Oh my god!

*The class are all running
about on the hard shoulder.*

Mr Jones   **Year 9! Year 9!
Get back here now!
All of you! Now!**

*Slowly they come back
to the bus.*

Policeman   We've been observing you
for some time, sir.
You've been swaying
all over the road.
Are you sure you're fit to drive?

Mr Jones	Of course I am.
	Look officer, I can explain.
	One of the class was feeling sick ...
	and there was this wasp ...
	and everyone was trying to duck ...
	and then we broke a window ...
	and then I ... I ... stopped!
Policeman	I see sir!
	Perhaps I'd better have
	a word with them.

Everyone is back by the bus now,
chattering away.
Right, listen up everyone!

They carry on talking.

Listen!

Again they carry on talking.

Policeman SHUT UP!

(*Silence*)

That's better.
Now there are two ways to do this.
There is your way,
and there is my way.
Your way – you carry on like this,
shouting, acting the fool,
a danger to yourselves
and everyone else –
and I take you straight back
to your school.
My way – you shut up and
start behaving yourselves –
and maybe, just maybe,
we'll let you go on to Denton Park.
Which is it to be?

Everyone	Your way.
Policeman	Right then! Listen!
	The motorway is a
	dangerous place,
	a very dangerous place.
	People get killed here.
	It is not a playground.
	So now we are going to
	be very careful,
	because there is a lot
	of broken glass around.
	We are going to
	put our seat belts on,
	and we are going on to
	Denton Park,
	where we will have a nice time
	on all the rides.
	Are we going to behave ourselves?

Everyone Yes!

Policeman And are we going to
listen to the teacher?

Everyone Yes!

Policeman Good!

*The **Policeman** closes the
minibus doors,
and turns to **Mr Jones**
who has been quietly fuming
through all this.*

A firm hand, sir!
That's all they need!

Mr Jones I know that, but ...

*Thinks better of it,
and grits his teeth.*

Yes, officer!
Thank you officer!

Policeman   You see sir, they're not bad kids,
but they need to be shown
who's boss.
I think you'll be all right now.
We'll follow you for a bit.

Mr Jones   Thank you officer.

He gets back in the minibus,
slams the door angrily,
and drives off.

Amy   That policeman was cross,
wasn't he sir?

Mr Jones   (*Still through gritted teeth*)
Yes, Amy.

Amy   He thought you were too soft,
didn't he sir?

Mr Jones   Maybe.

Amy	But I don't think he was fair, sir.
Mr Jones	Don't you, Amy?
Amy	No sir.
	People don't realise
	how hard it is being a teacher.
Mr Jones	Thank you Amy.
Kevin	Sir, sir!
Mr Jones	What is it now, Kevin?
Kevin	I'm feeling better now, sir.
	I thought you'd like to know.
Mr Jones	Good Kevin, I'm glad to hear it.
Adam	And sir ...
Mr Jones	Yes Adam?
Adam	The wasp has gone too!

***Mr Jones** drives on in silence!*

Act 3

The car park at Denton Park.
It is 3.30 in the afternoon
– time to go home.
The minibus has been repaired,
and everyone is waiting.

Kevin   Had a good time, sir?

Mr Jones Yes thank you, Kevin.

I didn't expect to,

after this morning,

but I have. What about you?

Kevin   Brilliant, sir!

The Death Ride was the best.

I was nearly sick on it.

Mr Jones That must have been good then.

What about the rest of you?

Everyone	Great sir ... Really good ...
	The best day out ever ...
	etc, etc.
Debbie	Did you go on the Death Ride sir?
Mr Jones	Yes I did, Debbie.
	I kept my eyes shut the whole
	time.
Debbie	We've got a picture of you
	on the log flume.
Mr Jones	Have you Debbie?
Debbie	Yes! You look really stupid, sir.
Mr Jones	Do I really?
Debbie	Yes, you're all wet,
	and you've got your mouth open,
	and your tongue hanging out.
Mr Jones	Have I?
Debbie	We're going to give it to
	Miss Smith.

Mr Jones	Well thank you for that, Debbie.
	I'm sure she'll find it very funny.
	(*To everyone*)
	Right then! Let's see if you're all here.
	One, two, three ...
	Stand still, Kevin ...
	six, seven, eight ...
	I said stand still ...
	... ten, eleven, twelve.
	Good, that's everybody.
Kevin	Sir, sir! Where's Adam?
Mr Jones	I don't know.
	He's here somewhere.
Kevin	He's not, sir.
Mr Jones	But he must be here.
	I've just counted twelve.
	Adam! Adam!

Kevin	He's not here, sir.
	He hasn't been here at all.
Mr Jones	But I could have sworn
	there were twelve …
	Never mind! Who was he with?
	Who saw him last?
Kevin	I was with him this morning,
	but then we split up.
Amy	I saw him in the queue
	for the Death Ride.
Mr Jones	When was that?
Amy	Hours ago.
Mr Jones	Has anybody seen him since?

(They all shake their heads)

Debbie	Wasn't there a big accident there
	I saw an ambulance
	and crowds of people.

Amy	Yes! Some kid was messing about, and fell off.
	He had to go to hospital.
Mr Jones	What?
Amy	I don't know if it was Adam.
Debbie	But it would be just like him.
	He's always doing stupid things like that.
Mr Jones	And was this accident this afternoon?
Amy	Yes!
Mr Jones	And no-one has seen him since.
Everyone	No!
Mr Jones	(*Starting to panic*)
	Oh no!
Kevin	Don't worry about Adam, sir.
	He's always breaking something.
	It's not your fault.
	If he hurts himself,
	no-one's going to blame you.

Mr Jones	You're a great comfort, Kevin, I must say.
Kevin	I mean just because you're supposed to be in charge, no-one's going to blame you just because Adam gets himself killed.
Mr Jones	Look, I could do without this, Kevin.
Kevin	Don't worry, sir. You won't get sacked.
Mr Jones	Will you be quiet, Kevin!
Kevin	Well, I was just trying to help.
Mr Jones	Let me think, let me think. Now, we must find out what's happened ... Amy, you go to the Death Ride, and ask there ...

Amy	Yes sir.
Mr Jones	Debbie, you go to the manager's office, and find out where they've taken him ...
Debbie	All right sir.
Mr Jones	Kevin, you'd better stay here ...
Kevin	OK sir.
Mr Jones	Now we need someone to ring up school and tell them.
Adam	I can do that.
Mr Jones	Good Adam. You do that and I'll ... ADAM???
Adam	What?
Everyone	(*Groaning*) Oh Adam! ... Adam you prat ... etc, etc.
Adam	Why? What's the matter?

Mr Jones	(*Angrily*)
	Where have you been?
Adam	Just here.
Mr Jones	But you weren't here a minute ago, were you?
Adam	No, I just got here.
Mr Jones	But why didn't you say anything?
Adam	I was wondering who you were looking for.
Mr Jones	Why weren't you here at 3.30?

Adam	I was on the Death Ride.
	I'd queued for hours.
	I wasn't going to miss it.
Mr Jones	Adam! We thought you'd
	had an accident.
	We were worried about you.
Adam	Were you sir? That's nice.
Mr Jones	But we were due to go at 3.30.
Adam	Yes sir, but I knew
	you wouldn't go without me.
Mr Jones	WHAT???

He steps forward as if to throttle **Adam***, then controls himself.*

	Adam! We shall talk about this
	again.
	Right everybody, one last check
	One, two, three ...
	stand still Kevin ...
Kevin	Yes sir.

Mr Jones	Six, seven . . .
	don't annoy me again Adam . . .
	eleven, twelve, thirteen,
	THIRTEEN???
	There can't be thirteen.
	Let's try again.
	One, two . . . . twelve, thirteen!
	But it can't be! It can't be!
Kevin	Yes, that's right sir.
	There were twelve before
	when you counted us,
	and now we've found Adam,
	that's thirteen.
Mr Jones	But . . . but only twelve
	came this morning.
	We can't have grown one.
	(*Trying to think clearly*)
	Right! Listen carefully.
Everyone	OK sir.

Mr Jones   Is there anyone who is here now
who should not be here now?

(*Silence*)

OK. Is there anyone who is not
here now who should be here now?
(*Everyone looks confused*)

Adam   (*Trying to be helpful*)
Nobody is not here now, sir.
Everybody is here now.

Mr Jones   No ... No ...
What I mean is ...
(*He takes a deep breath*)
Is there anyone who is here now,
and who is going home with us,
but who didn't come
with us this morning?

Emma   (*Stepping out from behind Amy*)
Me sir.

Mr Jones	EMMA???
	YOU???
Emma	Yes sir.
Mr Jones	What are you doing here?
Emma	Visiting Denton Park sir.
Mr Jones	I KNOW THAT!!!
	But you were banned!
	You were told, were you not,
	that you could not come
	to Denton Park with us!
Emma	Yes sir, I know.
	But I wasn't told I couldn't
	come back with you.
Mr Jones	What?
Emma	I was told I couldn't go to
	Denton Park with you.
	But I wasn't told I couldn't
	come back with you.

Mr Jones	But ... but ... how did you get here?
Emma	My dad gave me a lift. He's a lorry driver.
Mr Jones	But I can't take you back now.
Emma	Why not? There's enough room.
Mr Jones	Why not? You know why not! You've been banned!
Amy	You'll have to take her back now sir – her dad's gone on to Manchester.
Emma	She's right sir. So I've got to go back with you.
Amy	You can't leave her here.
Adam	Come on sir. Get a move on. We can't hang around here all day.
Mr Jones	Wha ...?

Emma	Hurry up sir!
	Chop chop!
Mr Jones	Chop chop???
Emma	Yes, I'm going out tonight.
	I need to get ready.
Mr Jones	(*Losing his temper*)
	WHAT???
Kevin	By the way sir?
Mr Jones	(*Just controlling himself*)
	Yes, Kevin.
Kevin	Where are you taking us next?

That's the final straw.
After everything that has
happened to him today,
Mr Jones *finally loses his temper.*

Mr Jones	WHY YOU CHEEKY …